I0437503

The Little Book of

BIG
QUOTATIONS

To Help FUEL
YOUR SUCCESS!

www.lulu.com

Copyright © 2008 Tami S. Easter

All rights reserved. No part of this book may be used or reproduced in any manor whatsoever without the written permission of the Publisher.

ISBN 978-1-4357-0844-0

Contents

Acknowledgements

I would like to acknowledge the following people:

My outstanding children! I am grateful for their support and encouragement throughout all of my professional endeavors.

Dr. Dwarka Ramphal one of the best instructors I have ever had, and my inspiration for continuous professional growth and development.

Petrina Bryant, a dear friend and amazing poet, who served as a sounding board throughout this project.

Special friends & family members – you know who you are - for providing continuing guidance, and support.

PARTICULARLY my big sister Paulette!

Especially my students for allowing me to touch their lives and encourage their success.

Introduction

*I*n teaching career development courses at a local college I began the practice of writing a quotation on the board before beginning each class. SOMETIMES it was to initiate conversation about the chapters we were covering, but EVERYTIME it was to invoke inspiration.

I found that my students looked forward to their "pearl" each day. So much so, that if ever we got off to a "rushed" start, and I omitted the quotation – someone would yell out, "HEY, WHERE'S OUR 'QUOTE' FOR TODAY?"

I came to realize that EVERYONE could use a push sometimes – that little extra something to remind us what we're striving for in our personal, and professional lives.

Before

WE

begin…

Take a

Moment to Reflect…

My current job/profession is:

_____

My family life consists of:

_____

_____

_____

The state of my financial situation is:

_____

_____

_____

My current education level is:

_____

_____

_____

My character can be described as:

_____

_____

_____

My general attitude is:

_____

_____

_____

_____

_____

Always plan ahead.
It wasn't raining when Noah
built the ark
- Richard C. Cushing

My short-term (within 1 year) goals are:

_____

_____

_____

_____

My mid-term (within 3-5 years) goals
are:

_____

_____

_____

_____

My long-term (within 10 years) goals are:

_____

_____

_____

_____

_____

_____

Mission

"Even if you are on the right track, you'll get run over if you just sit there."
- Will Rogers

The significance in asking yourself these questions is a GREAT determinant to your success. To not set goals for yourself in life is the same as getting in your car and driving around AIMLESSLY! You *could* reach your destination, but WHEN? Your "destination" could easily be passed by. And what about the waste in resources? In your car, it's your gas and still your time. But in life, it is a **WASTE OF** YOUR TIME, YOUR FINANCIAL RESOURCES, AND MOST OF ALL – **YOUR POTENTIAL!**

"Do not confuse motion and progress. A rocking horse keeps moving but does not make any progress."
- Alfred Montapert

In order to reach your full potential, you must first have direction. Once you have direction, you'll be **prepared** for the bumps along the road. You will find it easier to maintain YOUR FOCUS – YOUR DRIVE!

However, **without direction – you're** just wandering around AIMLESSLY – in motion, but **not progressing!**

We often discredit the value of our time. However, time is the most valuable resource that we have. We must REMEMBER that with EVERY passing minute, is a passing OPPORTUNITY! To be successful, you have to make the most of every moment. You must identify YOUR DIRECTION so that your life is not identified by aimless motion, but continuous progress!

The good life,
as I conceive it,
is a happy life.
I do not mean that if you are
good you will be happy;
I mean that if you are happy
you will be good.

- *Bertrand Russell*

A considerable part of finding your direction, is designing your mission statement. MOST LARGE AND SMALL ORGANIZATIONS HAVE A MISSION STATEMENT. **So should YOU!**

To help, I'll share **my** mission statement with you. From time to time I have to read it again – to remind myself what I aim for, stand for, and strive for.

Yours will help you too!

Mission Statement

I will work and play where my integrity cannot be compromised.

I will demonstrate character through trust, respect, responsibility, fairness, and citizenship.

I will continue to uphold high standards of honesty.

I will allow myself to empathize, not sympathize.

I will set and follow a good example everyday.

I will be committed to continual growth and learning throughout my life.

In everything I do, I shall give my interest, my devotion, my enthusiasm, my love, and most of all, myself.

Motivational Quotation:

"If better is possible, then good is not enough."
- Julian Harden

What is YOUR MISSION?

Ask yourself, "What is the legacy I want to leave behind?"

_____

_____

_____

_____

_____

_____

_____

_____

_____

"If you think you are too small to make a difference, try sleeping in a closed room with a mosquito."

- African Proverb

The *UNCONDITIONAL FIVE!*

S uccess is NOT LUCK! Success is EFFORT! There are basic principles that have been used time and time again by successful people.

Successful people follow these simple **UNCONDITIONAL** ACTIONS! And if you plan for success **YOU MUST**...

1. Check your ATTITUDE!

You may not always have control of every situation, but you should ALWAYS have control of your ATTITUDE! Your attitude sets the mood for your success, and how you approach everything in LIFE.

2. WORK AT IT!

Success is a series of progressive actions. The key word is *actions*. I usually tell my students that if you are looking for a job – then THAT IS your job. For the time being – your ACTUAL JOB IS TO FIND A JOB! You have to look for a job the same way you would wake up to go to work everyday. There is NO ROOM for laziness – success takes work!

3. WORK ON YOURSELF!

Recognize the constant need for self-improvement. Work on your skills, your knowledge, YOURSELF!

4. NEVER GIVE UP!

Understand that there will always be obstacles along the way. Do your best to think "outside the box." There is always a path to success – take your time to find it. It will come in its' own time with effort, but you will NEVER achieve success if you give up looking for it!

5. SEIZE EVERY OPPORTUNITY!

Everyday that you awake is a day FILLED with OPPORTUNITY! It will only be as productive as you make it. It is vital to your success that you **BE READY** and **PREPARED** to meet each and every opportunity you encounter.

Attitude

"A cloudy day is no match for a sunny disposition."

- William Arthur Ward

"If you can't change your fate, change your attitude."
        - Amy Tan

Your attitude sets the tone for your life. It sets the tone for how you perform, the effort you put into activities, and how you treat other people. What most people fail to realize is that your attitude is CONTAGIOUS! You will generally get as good as you give – either positive or negative!

If you intend to truly succeed – you have to seek positive situations, therefore DO NOT create negative energy. This starts with YOUR ATTITUDE!

"Ability is what you're capable of doing. Motivation determines what you do. Attitude determines how well you do it."
- Lou Holtz

Ask yourself, "What can I change about my attitude to cultivate my success?"

_____

_____

_____

_____

_____

_____

_____

_____

_____

Success

A person who aims at nothing is sure to hit it.

- Anonymous

"The only place where success comes before work is a dictionary."
- Vidal Sassoon

The truth in this statement is that in the dictionary – alphabetically – success does come before work. However, in REALITY YOU WILL NEVER REACH SUCCESS UNLESS YOU WORK FOR IT, and at it. Whatever your goals may be - you will only achieve success with hard work and true effort.

"Many of life's failures are people who did not realize how close they were to success when they gave up."
- Thomas A. Edison

Successful people **ARE NOT AFRAID** of failure. With every failed endeavor more experience, and learning opportunities are gained.

"I have not failed. I've just found 10,000 ways that won't work."
- Thomas Edison

To reach success you must never get discouraged, or even THINK about giving up.

KEEP TRYING!!!

Most importantly, you need to have a clear understanding of YOUR DEFINITION of success. Success is a relative term. For some success may be becoming a millionaire. For others it may be achieving executive status, becoming an entrepreneur, obtaining a promotion – there are different levels and ideas of success for everyone.

"Success is a journey, not a destination. The doing is often more important than the outcome."

- Arthur Ashe

Before you can begin your journey to success, you first need to KNOW WHERE YOU'RE TRYING TO GO!

Ask yourself, "What is MY DEFINITION of success?"

_____

_____

_____

_____

_____

_____

_____

_____

Character

"When your work speaks for itself, don't interrupt."
- Henry Kaiser

"Notice that the stiffest tree is most easily cracked, while the bamboo or willow survives by bending in the wind."
- Bruce Lee

Compromise! Compromise! Compromise! No one achieves success alone! It doesn't matter if it's expertise, financial resources, or networking contacts. At some point in time YOU WILL **NEED SOMETHING FROM SOMEONE!**

Understand that bending a little, does not have to compromise your character, integrity, OR authority. There will be times when the best outcome will only be achieved when a compromise is reached. ALWAYS strive for the BEST OUTCOME in every situation!

If you take care of your character, your reputation will take care of itself.
- American Proverb

Regardless of your profession, it will always be important to maintain your character and integrity. You never know when your reputation will stand in the way of your dream job, or sealing the deal of a lifetime.

"Character is like a tree and reputation like its shadow. The shadow is what we think of it; the tree is the real thing."
- Abraham Lincoln

Keep in mind that often it's necessary to do more than the minimum. You may find it necessary to occasionally assist a co-worker. Performing beyond your job description speaks volumes for your character, and your commitment to successful outcomes.

"What you do speaks so loudly that I cannot hear what you say."
- Ralph Waldo Emerson

Ask yourself, "What do my actions say about my character?"

"Is my character in line for success?"

_____

_____

_____

_____

_____

_____

_____

_____

_____

Self improvement

"Never confuse the size of your paycheck with the size of your talent."
  - Marlon Brando

As long as you are willing to strive for greatness, your possibilities are insurmountable. It is easy to become discouraged by current situations, but you have to be able to use these situations as growing opportunities. It is important to realize that where you are today, is in NO WAY A REPRESENTATION OF YOUR FUTURE, your potential, or the opportunities that lie ahead. SUCCESS IS UP TO YOU!

Be REALISTIC! Does your goal require you to return to school? Does it require relocation? What experience will you need to obtain? **What about your credit?** These are all questions that should guide you towards the beginning of making positive changes for yourself, and achieving your idea of success. Recognize that **bad credit** will not only prevent you from getting the car, or house you want, **but also the job, or business loan that you NEED**. Order copies of your credit reports and START REPAIRING YOUR CREDIT NOW!

"The man who doesn't read good books has no advantage over the man who can't read them."

- Mark Twain

Information is more powerful than you could imagine. In every business, profession, or career choice - changes in technology, laws, and practice will ALWAYS occur. Reading keeps you abreast and current with changing events. Subscribe to professional journals, join professional organizations – grow your knowledge! It is imperative to your success.

"Change your thoughts and you change your world."

- Norman Vincent Peale

Ask yourself, "What personal improvements can I make to promote my success?"

_____

_____

_____

_____

_____

_____

_____

_____

Opportunity

"If opportunity doesn't knock, build a door."
- Milton Berle

"A pessimist sees the difficulty in every opportunity; an optimist sees the opportunity in every difficulty."
   -Sir Winston Churchill

Opportunity is in line with Attitude – each opportunity you have will be EXACTLY what you make of it. Each opportunity has the potential to be a positive experience, but what will you make out of it? It's completely up to you!

"You can't build your reputation on what you're going to do.
   - Henry Ford

Many people CREATE their own opportunities. Action! Action! Action! Take charge of your future! If you KNOW what your aspirations are then you are MOST QUALIFIED to captain your ship! A dream will always be a dream, but action makes it reality!

"It is better to be prepared for an opportunity and not have one than to have an opportunity and not be prepared."
- Whitney Young Jr.

Ask yourself, "How can I best prepare myself to capitalize on every opportunity?"

_____

_____

_____

_____

_____

_____

_____

Excuses

Excuses are tools of incompetence that build monuments of nothingness and those that insist upon using them are seldom good at anything else.
    - Anonymous

"He that is good at making excuses is seldom good at anything else."
- Benjamin Franklin

It is only NATURAL to find excuses for the lack of progress.   The truth is that excuses fuel digression, not progression.   Please understand that EVERY EXCUSE is an OBSTACLE towards your success.

Ask yourself, "What are my obstacles?" "And, how can I defeat them?"

_____

_____

_____

_____

_____

_____

_____

Perseverance

"Big shots are only little shots who keep shooting."
- Christopher Morely

"It's not whether you get knocked down, it's whether you get up."
- Vince Lombardi

It is important to accept failure as a path to success. Statistically, most flourishing entrepreneurs failed at their FIRST attempts at becoming successful business owners. It is vital to remember that each failure is an opportunity to try again, and if you CHOSE NOT TO TRY – then and - **only then** will you truly fail!

"To avoid criticism, do nothing, say nothing, be nothing."
- Elbert Hubbard

Don't be afraid of what others may say about your ideas. Where would the world be today without the inventions of Benjamin Franklin, Alexander Graham Bell, or Thomas Edison? Regardless of how unconventional their ideas may have seemed - it never stopped their pursuits. Learn to **EXPECT** criticism, and prepare to grow from it!

Today is the day to seize your opportunity!

Ask yourself, "How can I aim for success today?"

_____

_____

_____

_____

_____

_____

_____

_____

_____

Yesterday is a cancelled check. Tomorrow a promissory note. Today is ready cash. How are you going to spend it?
*   - Unknown*

Regardless of your life's path - *TO BE SUCCESSFUL* - you **MUST PLAN YOUR WORK** – then **WORK YOUR PLAN!**

What's your PLAN?

How are you going to change careers, OR improve your PROFESSIONAL situation? What steps are you going to take?

_____

_____

_____

_____

_____

_____

_____

_____

What's your PLAN?

How are you going to change, or improve your FAMILY/PERSONAL situation? What steps are you going to take?

_____

_____

_____

_____

_____

_____

_____

_____

_____

_____

_____

_____

What's your PLAN?

How are you going to change, or improve your FINANCIAL situation? What steps are you going to take?

_____

_____

_____

_____

_____

_____

_____

_____

_____

_____

_____

_____

_____

"I've missed more than 9000 shots in my career. I've lost almost 300 games. 26 times, I've been trusted to make the game winning shot and missed. I've failed over and over again in my life. And that is why I succeed."
- Michael Jordan

EVERYTHING YOU WANT IN LIFE IS WAITING FOR YOU TO REACH FOR IT! **GOOD LUCK!**

Please address your thoughts/comments to:

Tami S. Easter, M.A., M.B.A., PHR
Training Director,

Training Wills
P.O. Box 12364
Wilmington, NC 28405
www.TrainingWills.net

www.ingramcontent.com/pod-product-compliance
Lightning Source LLC
Chambersburg PA
CBHW031333290526
45784CB00014B/2624